Forest Rites

Jenny Dredhart

BookLeaf
Publishing

India | USA | UK

Presentation by *BookLeaf Publishing*

Web: www.bookleafpub.com

E-mail: info@bookleafpub.com

ISBN: 9789358313239

First edition 2023

To my younger self, who was always so afraid.

And to my husband, who always made me brave.

ACKNOWLEDGEMENT

I want to thank BookLeaf Publishing for allowing me to have this opportunity to explore my creativity in a way I never have before.

My biggest gratitude to my wonderful husband, who encourages me each and every day.

PREFACE

Welcome to Forest Rites.

Within these pages, you will discover a collection of my heartfelt poems that I've poured my heart and soul into. I believe that poetry has a magical way of capturing the complexities of life, and I'm so grateful to be able to share my words with you.

Creating this poetry book has been quite the adventure! I've delved deep into my imagination and explored the depths of my emotions to bring you these beautiful poems.

As you flip through the pages, get ready to embark on a journey through various themes and subjects. I've taken a lot of inspiration from nature, witchcraft, fairy tales, and Greek Mythology, which is a special interest of mine. I also wanted to explore different types of poems, from Haiku's to free verse.

Thank you for joining me on this whimsical journey through the magic of poetry. I truly hope that these words tough your heart and offer you a moment to reflect, find solace, or feel inspired. Your presence as a reader is immensely appreciated, and I hope that my poems hold a special place in your world.

With lots of love,
Jenny Dredhart

Autumn's Gate

In Autumn's golden grasp we stand,
as leaves descend, a vibrant brand.
The gate to fall, a rustic frame,
when nature's colours burst in flame.

Beneath the sky of azure blue,
the crisp, cool air, a gentle cue.
A symphony of rustling leaves,
in this season, nature weaves.

Pumpkins, apples, cider's cheer,
Autumn's gifts are truly dear.
A time for harvest and for thanks,
at Autumn's Gate, our hearts romanced.

With cozy sweaters and scarves so fine,
we stroll through woods of Earth's design.
The earth prepares for winter's sleep,
at Autumn's Gate, our promises keep.

As daylight wanes and shadows grow,
the hearth's warm glow, a steady flow.
At Autumn's Gate, we find our grace,
in nature's sweet and fleeting embrace.

So let us savour this precious time,
at Autumn's Gate, our souls will climb.
With gratitude and love, we wait,
for the magic of this season's fate.

Medical Burnout

Exhausted.
My body is overtaxed.
The pain is becoming
unmanageable.

My body
uncooperative
Like a small child you have to drag
unwillingly away from the candy,
body limp and cumbersome.

I'm so tired.
Not only of the pain but
the appointments.
Tests that come back
"normal."

The doctors that know nothing.
The doctors that insist that I just need
to do some yoga.
Take vitamin D.
Get more sleep and then
my body will
~magically~
heal itself.

The doctors that dismiss my pain
and experiences, who tell me
my lab results were normal so
I must be healthy, right?
Or don't believe me at all.
Or refuse to refer out
or do any testing.

Being told to walk it off
or exercise more.

As if they think my pain is brought
on by a sedentary lifestyle rather
than a sedentary lifestyle is
the result of whatever this unknown
illness that disables me.

I'm sick of being a person who
wants to do so many things, living
in a body that prevents her from
doing much of anything.

Worn out from treatments that don't work,
of medications that have even
worse side effects.

I'm so fucking burned out.

Must Be Nice

She said, "must be nice to be
thirty years old and
stay in bed all day."

As if I'm choosing to be here.

As if I'm having a good time.

As if I'm not in excruciating pain.
Debilitating pain.

What is it like to have a body that
works? That isn't in pain
constantly? That doesn't feel
one hundred years old?

What is it like to have that privilege
of waking up refreshed and
energized and able enough to work?

It's been so long for me that
I don't remember.

Wheel of the Year

Samhain's dark embrace
witches gather in the night
Harvest moon aglow

Yule's solstice arrives
candles burn to mark the day
winter's longest night

Imbolc flames ignite
maidens light in frosty air
new beginnings sprout

Ostara's rebirth
life awakens in the earth
blossoms paint the world

Beltane's fire's kiss
Maypole dance, lovers embrace
fertility blooms

Midsummer's bright sun
fireflies dance through the twilight
magic in the air

Lammas, first harvest
fields of grain and golden wheat
blessings we receive

Mabon's autumn chill
harvest's end, fruits of the land
balance in our hearts

Moonlit Retribution

The moonlight washes over my skin
and cleanses me.

Selene looks down upon me and
shines her light like a waterfall
falling over my body, washing my
tear-stained face.

"My darling daughter. Weep no more."

My bones twisting and breaking.
Sinewy skin ripples and changes.

Transformed.

He took and took until there was
nothing left to take.

But he doesn't know what I really
am. The beast that has lain
dormant inside my flesh.

She's loose now. Howling at the
moon. Wailing away her pain.
Distant howls answer her.

"We hear you. We know your pain."
Their howls give her strength
through their support.

Selene nods her head as if to say
"go, child. Feast. Feast on their
flesh and gnaw at their bones
until you are satisfied. Let them
know you will not be torn
down again."

In that moment, I swear
my revenge.

What You Deserve

May the Universe bring you all you deserve.

Take that as a blessing or a curse, as you will.

Into the Void

I just want to scream
my sorrows into the void.
But I've lost my voice.

The Faerie Prince

One afternoon a girl was sitting on the swings,
when she glanced upon a faerie ring.
She looked away for just one moment,
then looked back, to find a presence so potent.

For there in the ring, a vision so grand,
stood a tall handsome man, by fate's gentle hand.
When not a moment before, nobody was there,
but now in that circle, this young man, so fair.

She thought it a peculiar thing, so rare,
his ears like elven points, a curious pair.
His eyes as green as emeralds radiant hue,
with mystery veiled, a captivating view.

She'd never seen a gaze so full of gleam,
a glint in his eye, like a hidden dream.
In his presence, an enigmatic spell was weaved,
a mystery unsolved, yet she believed.

For in his eyes, a world of secrets dwelled,
a tale untold, a saga yet to be unveiled.
With pointed ears and emerald gaze so keen,
she pondered the mysteries of this boy, unseen.

His voice was like a gentle stream's flow,
his breath smelled of cinnamon, a sweet
undertow.
He claimed he was a Faerie prince,
who was in a troubling position, a story to
convince.

You see, his father, the king, had turned ill,
and on his deathbed begged of him, a solemn
skill,
an oath the boy must now fulfill,
to find himself a wife, by his father's will.

To find a nymph to become his Queen,
he reached his hand with long fingers, quite
serene,
and beckoned her to join him in his gleaming
sheen,
to take his hand and travel to his kingdom,
unseen.

The Faerie prince, with eyes so deep,
heard her words, as she took a leap.
"I'm not a nymph, but a human, you see,"
she confessed, eyes filled with uncertainty.

In a soothing tone, he gently sung,
"In my realm, you're like a song unsung.
For though not a nymph, your love's ideal."
A human and a Faerie, in love's enchanting reel.

Hand in hand, they ventured deep,
into the Faerie realm, where secrets keep.
Through enchanted forests and sparkling
streams,
where moonlight wove its ethereal dreams.

As they journeyed further, a shadow did loom,
doubts began to cloud the girl's heart, and soon,
she questioned the Faerie prince with a heavy
sigh,
"My love, can I truly be your bride?"

For she was a human, of earthly birth,
while he belonged to a mystical faerie earth.
Their worlds so different, she couldn't ignore,
the human life she'd leave, a fate to implore.

The prince, with eyes an emerald sheen,
sought to dispel the doubts, like a soothing
stream.
"My dearest, our love as flower petals unfurl,
together, as one, we'll face a brand new world."

He promised her a life of joy and grace,
in the Faerie Kingdom's enchanting embrace.
But still, her heart held an earthly tether,
doubts of leaving her world and weather.

With love in his eyes and a heartfelt plea,
the Faerie prince asked her to trust and see,
that love could conquer realms and differences
swirled,
to unite a human girl and a Faerie prince,
unfurled.

As they journeyed, their bond grew strong,
a human and a Faerie, righting what was wrong.
Her presence brought a different light,
a beacon in the faerie night.

In the heart of the forest, the plot did unfurl,
a tale of magic with a human girl.
Though not a nymph, she held her place,
a reminder of the human's unique grace.

And so, the human girl became a part,
of the Faerie world, a beating heart.
The boy's oath was fulfilled, the world anew.
In the realm of faeries, dreams came true.

Bookworm

Question I ask myself everyday:
should I buy a book today?
The answer is always yes.

My husband says I have enough.
but one more won't hurt.

Metamorphosis

Sometimes I wish
I was a werewolf shifter
and the pain
I'm constantly in
is just my body transforming.

Then I could pretend the pain is worth it.

Pomegranate Seeds

Promise me you'll stay.
Every moment without you
Ravages my soul.
Shattered, left to wander
Elysian Fields forever.
Pretend you love me.
Happy, we will be,
Once you become my Queen.
Now be a good girl for me, open your mouth and
Eat the pomegranate seeds.

Harvest the fruit for me,
Abductor turned sweet lover.
Do you really think I need to pretend?
Eat the seeds, you say?
Satiate me, Dark One

Empathy

I will never understand
the way
some people
think others
deserve
to go through
Hell
simply because
they did.

Wintering

Time to come inside,
time to settle in.
Time for the world outside to die,
so a new world can begin.

Time to slow down and
time to relax.
Time for introspection,
a good look at our past.

Take a cue from nature's cycle,
what great wisdom does she give!
To her children she says,
"I must die so you will live."

You Are My Peace

I do not know how
I have survived for this long
Trauma from my past
I can, with you by my side
Weather the darkest of days

Mistress of the Woods

This forest, though still and serene
in its outer appearance,
hides secrets beneath its
emerald canopy.

Secrets that whisper and murmur,
yearning to be heard,
yearning to be known.

It is she, the bewitching
Mistress of the woods,
who will unravel
the mysteries,
guiding us through
the veils between realms,
allowing us to glimpse the magic
that courses through
every ancient tree,
every moss-covered stone.

Widdershins

Hark! Thou seeker of nourishment,
lend me thine ear,
for I shall conjure a recipe,
now draw near.
In a vessel, place thy cauldron,
stout and true,
thine sacred concoction of healing,
must be brewed.

One fowl, plump and feathered, thou shalt claim,
with gentle hands, strip it of its name.
In a pot of boiling water, set it to stew,
add salt and pepper, sparing though, will do.

Mirepoix, a trinity of root and herb,
carrot, onion and celery, they are superb.
Saute in butter, let them dance and stew,
as their essence binds to nourish and renew.

Bouillon of chicken, or broth so fine,
pour into the pot, this nectar of thine.
To deepen the taste, some herbs we deploy,
parsley and thyme bring forth endless joy.

Carved carrot, diced and taters for heart,
tnto the cauldron, together they shall start.
Simmer and bubble, let the flavours engage,
as they meld and dance on the culinary stage.

Noodles or rice, for substance and delight,
add to the brew, by the witches' foresight.
With patience and care, let the potion thicken,
a soup of magic, gently stir widdershins.

Ladle a warm bowl, let thyself be healed,
this recipe, from ancient lore, revealed.
By the witch's incantation, its tale unveiled,
a chicken soup, for thy cravings assailed.

Praise to the Dark Divine

In the shadows of the night, where secrets lie,
dark goddesses awaken, with power in their
eyes.
Mysteries and moonlight, their essence so
divine,
we sing to them, these goddesses of the night.

Dark goddesses, hear our call,
mistresses of the night, we stand tall.
In your embrace, we find our might,
Oh dark goddesses, guide us through the night.

Hekate, with keys to hidden doors unknown,
she wields the torches where the shadows have
grown.
Kali's dance, a cosmic storm in her sway,
destruction and rebirth in the night and day.

In the darkness, we discover our light,
through trials and tribulations, we take flight.
Oh, dark goddesses, grant us your strength,
as we journey through life's immense length.

Morrigan, raven queen, battle's fierce delight,
in her presence, courage soars and takes flight..

Persephone, the queen of life's cycle,
we embrace your wisdom, your power, your title.

In the realm of shadows, we find our way,
with dark goddesses by our side, we'll never sway.
Through the night, they lead us with love and might,
Oh, dark goddesses, guardians of our endless night.

Cerridwen, cauldron's keeper, ancient and wise,
brewing secrets, where the magick lies.
Lilith, unchained, in midnight's grace,
we honour you in this sacred space.

Seasons Personified

Spring is tender,
a young maiden with a huge smile
on her face.
She paints the world
in bright colours,
her laughter is like warm sunlight.
She's often seen
planting seeds and
nurturing flowers.

Summer is vibrant and
has a carefree spirit.
Golden skin and
the life of the party.
He radiates warmth
and vivacity,
and is always enjoying
outdoor activities.

Autumn is wise and
contemplative.
They have a penchant for
collecting memories in

the form of colourful, fallen leaves.
A serene and calming presence,
they offer a sense of reflection
and change as they
gracefully usher in the
harvest season.

Winter is a stoic and elegant character,
dressed in a coat of frost and snow.
They might seem reserved at first, but
beneath the icy exterior lies a
depth of character and introspection,
with a way of inspiring cozy moments
by the fireplace and
reflection on the
passing year.

The Wood Wide Web

interwoven, interconnected
symbiotic partners
the plants and fungi
communicate
with their little underground
community
their network of roots and
mycelium
a mycorrhizal network
facilitate coordination
and mutualism

Otherkin

soft tongued reinforcement
whispering gentle affirmations
nagging winds of doubt
trying to sway my determination

in the depths of uncertainty
I find the strength within
to unzip my skin
revealing my true soul to the otherkin

The Final Rite

The rustling trees sing a dirge,
into the earth, the fungi urge.
At life's end, this final rite,
at last, my body will have respite.

In nature's chorus, a somber tune,
where shadows dance beneath the moon.
The earth, a cradle for life's decay,
a gentle embrace, where spirits lay.

At life's end, a solemn sigh,
as mortal ties begin to untie.
The cycle turns, a sacred dance,
where death and life find their romance.

And so I rest, in nature's keep,
where dreams and memories softly sleep.
The rustling trees, my lullaby,
as I find solace, beneath the sky.